MW00535343

CUBE

50 Years of the World's Most Famous Cube

Roland Hall

WHITE
LION

CONTENTS

⬇ The biggest cube mosaic ever: *Macau Skyline*, 2010 (see pages 120–121).

FOREWORD

In loco parentis

Dear Reader,

In fifty years, I have been almost everywhere: from remote villages in the jungle to sleek executive offices in dazzling skyscrapers. People have taken me to the stratosphere and to the bottom of the ocean. People jumped out of airplanes with me while parachuting to the ground. Magicians awed their audiences with me, professors brought me to class and research; musicians dedicated their songs to me. I have inspired architects, engineers, computer programmers and designers. At the hands of skilful young enthusiasts, I have become a robust global sports phenomenon. I have even featured in countless movies and have been on the cover of thousands of magazines and hundreds of books discussing every topic under the sun.

This little book provides a colourful snapshot of my amazing adventures. Immerse yourself in the magical history of half a century.

On behalf of the Cube,

Ernő Rubik
Budapest, 2024.

INTRODUCTION

**Fifty years can really fly by . . .
when you've got a Cube to solve!**

It does not seem like such a long time ago that the Rubik's® Cube first hit the shelves and took over the world. Everyone – and we mean *everyone* – of a certain age will remember when they first encountered a Cube. It could have been at school, a party, a family gathering, but at some point we all became aware of the existence of this magical, puzzling object with six colours and an intuitive mechanic (you just knew what to do with it straight away).

At school, it was a source of camaraderie, competition and pride. At home, it was a fun puzzle for all the family. In popular culture, it became the symbol of an era.

And the Rubik's® Cube changed the world. Not just the world of puzzles and toys, its shape (and we don't just mean a cube, we mean an actual Rubik's® Cube), its colours and its name appeared in design magazines, music videos, architecture, street art, lessons at school and university – and more.

The Rubik's® Cube is so much more than the sum of its parts, and this book celebrates the many, many aspects of this design innovation that – amazingly – has already lasted half a century in its original form. Here's to all you solvers, cubers, hobbyists and casual owners hoping for another fifty years!

➜ A few faces of the Cube (clockwise from top): Educational puzzle solving involving art, Hungarian postage stamp, fun brand design, 50th Anniversary special edition Rubik's® Cube.

ORIGINS OF THE CUBE

The story begins with Ernő Rubik, in the city of Budapest, Hungary, in 1974 . . .

Professor Rubik had long held an interest in three-dimensional shapes as part of his work and also at home, and it was in his mother's house that his first cube was constructed: a series of wooden blocks first held together with elastic and paper clips. Rubik wanted to create something new and original, something never seen before: a piece of design art. And at first, when the blocks moved, the elastic snapped, leading Rubik to search for another way of holding the pieces together. The prototype was marked with symbols and shapes to show the 'home' position of each part. Through twisting and rotating, the cube could be rearranged; by the same process it could be reassembled. And so the Rubik's Cube was born. Rubik applied for a patent in Hungary in 1975, for a 'three-dimensional logical toy'. It was granted in 1977, and the first Cubes – known as *Büvös Kocka* ('Magic Cube') – went on sale in Hungary by the end of the year. Over three hundred thousand were sold there in a two-year period.

What followed is an extraordinary story of global sucess for a one-man creation from a small, central European, Communist country. The newly named 'Rubik's Cube' was the winner of the

➡ Professor Ernő Rubik making a promotional appearance, *c.*1982.

10

'What really interested me was not the nature of the Cube, but the nature of people, the relationship between people and the Cube.'

Ernő Rubik

prestigious Spiel des Jahres award in 1980 in Germany, leading to wider notoriety. The rest is history: one hundred million Cubes were sold over the next three years alone. It wasn't long before this worldwide phenomenon was everywhere: children, adults, teenagers, business people, all were solving Cubes – or at least attempting to. Books were published, competitions were set up and the Rubik's Cube became one of the cultural emblems of the 1980s, forever associated with the decade by those that lived through it and those that look back upon it. It was also a brilliant puzzle!

Pulitzer Prize-winning author and computer scientist Douglas Hofstadter, called the Rubik's Cube 'an ingenious mechanical invention, a pastime, a learning tool, a source of metaphors, an inspiration.' It was all of that, and more.

↑ Two early wooden prototypes of the 'Magic Cube', as it became known.

← Professor Rubik surrounded by many of his – solved – Rubik's Cubes.

CUBE
COMPETITIONS

It was not long after the Cube's establishment as a global puzzle craze that people started to take solving times seriously.

The first Rubik's Cube World Championship took place in 1982, at the height of the puzzle's original craze. It was held, of course, in Hungary, and Professor Rubik was in attendance. Cubers from all over the world attended and records were made and broken, notably the fastest solving time.

The new record was a blistering – unbelievably fast at the time – 22.95 seconds, posted by Minh Thai from Los Angeles, California, USA (see page 67). It's hard to believe that fifty years later the fastest solvers would be able to solve seven cubes in that time. Other famous and subsequently influential cube solvers present at that first gathering were Jessica Fridrich and Lars Petrus.

The World Championship was not repeated until 2003, after which it become a biannual event.

A governing body, The World Cube Association, was founded in 2004, and since that time competitions have been staged in more than 150 regions of the world, involving more than two hundred thousand competitors.

As of 2024, winners of the Rubik's WCA World Championships have hailed from the USA, France, Japan, the United Kingdom, Poland, Germany and Australia.

The event, of course, did not take place in 2021 due to the Covid-19 pandemic, but in August 2023, in South Korea, Max Park triumphed in the 3x3 cube category (the headline event), with an *average* solving time of 5.31 seconds.

In the first competition in 1982, the fastest speed won, but current rules state that each contestant has to solve a cube five times. The fastest and slowest times are omitted, and the mean of the three remaining times is calculated and used.

⬉ The very first Cube world championships, in Budapest in 1982.

⬆ A 2014 Cube competition in Houston, Texas, USA.

FASTEST CUBE SOLVES

Solving times represent a great example of humankind's ability to solve problems – and then want to solve them quicker!

Cube solving has come a long way since Professor Rubik managed to get his wooden prototype back to its original state. As you can see from the chart opposite, times have plummeted since the first world championships.

We've only included the fastest 3x3 cube solving time, but there are records for every puzzle cube type and many event categories. The World Cube Association keeps an up-to-date list of times, competitors and categories online, so you can check if you are getting close to a time that will get you into the list of the world's fastest solvers. If you are, you'd best get along to an authorized gathering and put your skills to the test . . .

However, the competition is incredibly stiff and the gaps at the top are tight. For example, Yiheng Wang has nine sub-4-second cube solves to his name and still doesn't sit at the top of the rankings for 3x3 solving. (That honour goes to world record holder Max Park.)

As we'll see later, computers and robots can solve the cube in the blink of an eye, but with solving times getting ever smaller, it may not be long before a human achieves a sub-3-second time.

You'd better warm up your fingers (see page 96), get your timer ready and make sure you are using nothing but the fastest algorithms (see page 78) and finger tricks (see page 150). Good luck!

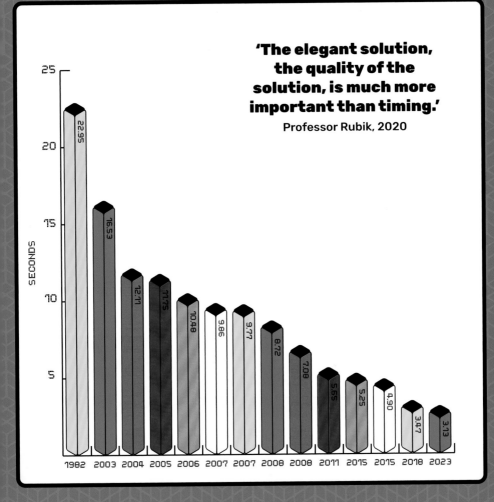

'The elegant solution, the quality of the solution, is much more important than timing.'

Professor Rubik, 2020

SECONDS

25

20

15

10

5

22.95 1982
16.53 2003
12.11 2004
11.75 2005
10.48 2006
9.86 2007
9.77 2007
8.72 2008
7.08 2008
5.65 2011
5.25 2015
4.90 2015
3.47 2018
3.13 2023

3.13
SECONDS

'At that time [1997], an average of 13 seconds seemed as unachievable as travelling to Mars.'

Jessica Fridrich

CUBE CALCULATIONS

We know that there is a vast number of variations possible on a cube, and that there is only one single correct state (when all the colours are lined up).

And there is a common – and mistaken – belief that you can simply solve a Cube by fiddling around a bit, again and again. Nobody who has used a Cube for more than a few minutes will believe that is possible. For a start, the 43 quintillion variations will take you multiple lifetimes to go through. If you turned the Rubik's Cube's sides randomly, you could spend your whole life turning one side per second and there would be no guarantee you would ever get it back to its original state.

This is one of the reasons the Cube is admired by mathematicians: many fascinating mathematical principles can be applied to the Cube itself. Books have been written about the maths associated with it.

It may seem that the Cube is infinitely puzzling, but in fact the six colours, nine squares and limited (albeit large) number of moves means calculations are manageable.

Mathematics, theory, algorithms and discussion of particles, quarks and baryons seem to have started shortly after the Cube came out in

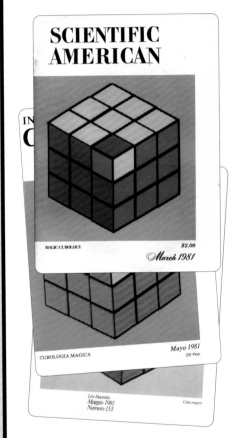

SCIENTIFIC AMERICAN

IN
C

MAGIC CUBOLOGY $2.00
                          March 1981

CUBOLOGIA MAGICA   *Mayo 1981*
                              250 Ptas.

Live Duemila
Maggio 1981   *Cubo magico*
Numero 153

the USA. Douglas R. Hofstadter's famous article in *Scientific American*, 'Metamagical Themas' discussed all of them, and even included a diagram showing how to take the 'Magic Cube' to pieces and reassemble it. That demonstrates the practical difference between cube theory (it is solvable through mathematics and manipulation) and cube practice (let's take it to bits and put it back together).

Astonishingly, *any* scrambled Rubik's Cube can be solved in a maximum 20 moves. That is known as God's Number and was discovered by a team of mathematicians – Tomas Rokicki, Herbert Kociemba, Morley Davidson and John Dethridge – following many years of careful, computer-crunching research.

SMALL-SCREEN CUBE

The Rubik's Cube has become without a doubt a symbol of the 1980s, but it has regularly featured on television screens ever since.

Back in that first decade of popularity there was an entire animated show, *Rubik, the Amazing Cube*. It was a Saturday-morning show for children that was first broadcast in 1983 and featured the adventures of a magical talking Cube, his three young friends and the many challenges they overcome.

There were also plenty of Rubik's Cube commercials made, many of them humorous – for example, 'Sure, Sir Isaac Newton unravelled the mysteries of gravity, but could he have unravelled the mysteries of Rubik's Cube?' They can be found online – have fun looking!

But the Rubik's Cube is representative of more than just an era: it is used on screen to depict a toy, a puzzle, familiar colours and patterns that reach back across the decades – and a sign of intelligence.

The Rubik's Cube has been featured in episodes of many television shows, you'll find a few key appearances overleaf . . .

➜ A celebrity escape room with a giant cube for 2020's Red Nose Day on US television.

THE BIG BANG THEORY

As you would expect from a show about geeky, intelligent people, *The Big Bang Theory* made frequent references to the Rubik's Cube over its twelve seasons. Ernő Rubik even sent the show a video message of thanks when it wound up, drawing attention to nerds 'like us'. The Cube is also seen in *Young Sheldon*.

THE SIMPSONS

The Rubik's Cube has made numerous appearances, usually as an indicator of high intellect. Episodes include 'Hurricane Neddy', 'HOMR', 'Frink Gets Testy', 'Mathlete's Feet' and 'Homer Defined' – where a sign of Homer's newly developed high IQ is his ability to quickly solve a basket of Rubik's Cubes.

DOCTOR WHO

The Rubik's Cube has made a few appearances in *Doctor Who*, most notably when the Eleventh Doctor is unable to solve a Cube he finds in a bedroom ('must be broken') while helping a family ('Night Terrors'). The same Doctor also has a Rubik's Cube in 'The God Complex' episode.

WEDNESDAY

Wednesday Addams had a black-and-white Rubik's Cube that Thing attempted to solve one-handed (of course). In fact, the Rubik's Icon was a real Cube, released in 2007, with sides that were white, black, silver and varying shades of grey.

← *The Tonight Show with Jay Leno* in 2010 – a one-hand Rubik's Cube solve while playing trumpet!

THE MILLION-DOLLAR CUBE

Of the many millions of cubes that have been constructed over the years, most follow a pattern: they have six colours (or patterns/shades/designs), are movable, solvable and portable.

This is part of what makes a Rubik's Cube a Rubik's Cube. And although there have been many special editions, Cubes have usually been created for the purpose of playing with as a puzzle.

Until the 'Masterpiece Cube'. In 1995, Diamond Cutters International (DCI) decided to create a one-of-a-kind cube from precious metal and gemstones. DCI's CEO, Fred Cuellar – a longtime fan – built the custom cube himself in collaboration with Rubik's. It is a scaled version of its mass-produced cousins, but it does weigh considerably more!

The sides are made with amethysts, rubies, diamonds, sapphires and emeralds, all of which are set into cubies made of gold. There are 25 gems in each small square.

The cube is fully functioning and is valued at around $2.5 million (£2 million), making the Masterpiece Cube not only the most expensive cube in the world (by some distance), but also the most expensive puzzle in the world.

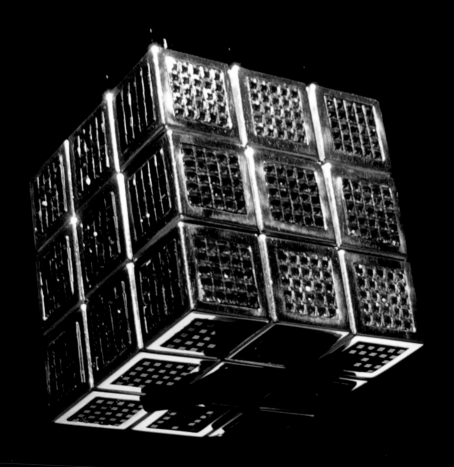

A HUGE NUMBER OF CUBES

When the first 'Magic Cubes' came off the production line in Hungary in 1977 it was not long before it became clear that the puzzle was hugely appealing to a wide variety of people, not only children. Professor Rubik famously spotted adults caught up in the fun of puzzle solving. But when the Cube's popularity spread from Rubik's homeland to the rest of the world, nobody could have imagined its success and popularity.

It is estimated that more than 450 million Cubes have been made and sold around the world – and the number keeps growing as each new generation discovers the thrill of the cube challenge and (hopefully) the satisfaction of solving it.

450,000,000
cubes sold around the world

INFINITE POSSIBILITIES?

When you start with a Rubik's Cube and scramble it for the first time, it may feel like you are never going to get it back together. But do you know how many combinations there are on that six-sided object? Some of these numbers may surprise you, even make you gasp, but don't worry . . .

Learning to solve is a great intellectual challenge and once you learn a few algorithms you will be flying. Don't let the numbers put you off. On the contrary, you'll have something to celebrate: 'Of the 43 quintillion-plus combinations possible I restored my Rubik's Cube to the only right one!'

43 quintillion,
252 quadrillion, 3 trillion,
274 billion, 489 million,
856 thousand =
possible permutations
of a Rubik's Cube.

AROUND THE WORLD

The Rubik's Cube has always been a language-free, culture-free puzzle. It can be solved by the very young and the very old, regardless of location.

It is likely that one of the reasons for the speed of success of the puzzle was that it was instantly recognizable by anyone. You did not need to ask if someone was using a Rubik's Cube, it was obvious because there was nothing else like it in the world. Not long after the first Rubik's Cubes came out internationally, children and adults all over the world were spotted twisting away with them.

It was possible to teach someone to solve the Rubik's Cube without using words – you could simply show them the moves. And the puzzle could be solved in a group, with many solving together at the same time, or you could solve solo and compare notes with your fellow cubers afterwards. From Japan to Jamaica and from Alaska to Argentina, the Rubik's Cube was everywhere.

➜ Young people discover the joy of Cube solving with a Rubik's Speed Cube.

⬇ Cube solvers from around the world, through fifty years of puzzling.

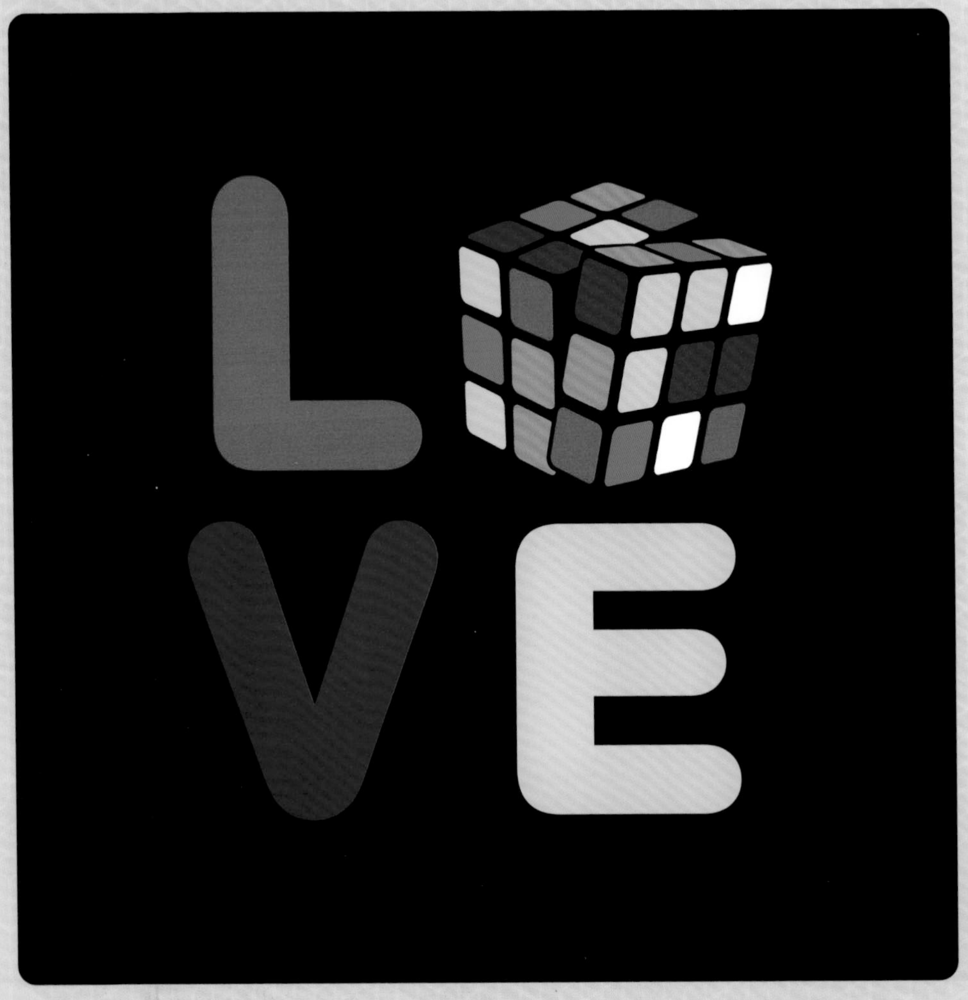
L
VE

DESIGN
INNOVATION

#10

The Rubik's Cube was built to Rubik's own unique design. The problem he encountered was how to keep the shape of the Cube and enable the rotation of (nearly) all the parts, while not allowing the object to fall to pieces. As you can see from the image below, a seemingly simple construction of overlaps allow this to happen. The central blocks (fixed) hold the other pieces in place but let them rotate.

Tiny nodes on the cubies are designed to hold them together in one structure while the sides and layers are being turned.

The Rubik's Cube has been featured in design magazines and courses.

← A deconstructed Cube, clearly showing the important nodes that hold the structure together.

→ Diagrams from Professor Rubik's original patent in the USA, dated 1983.

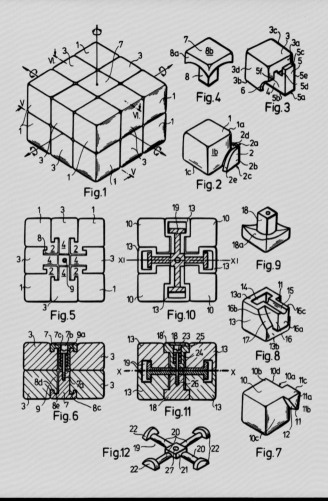

Fig.1

Fig.4

Fig.3

Fig.2

Fig.5

Fig.10

Fig.9

Fig.8

Fig.6

Fig.11

Fig.7

Fig.12

39

SOLVING: BEGINNER'S METHOD

#11

Here is the most basic solution to solving the Rubik's Cube – in other words, the easiest solution. This method involves learning the fewest algorithms and is therefore the quickest to learn.

Although it is by no means the fastest solution, it is tried and tested, and has been in circulation in various iterations for nearly as long as the Cube itself.

This is currently the method that is recommended by the makers of the Rubik's Cube, and with hundreds of millions enjoyed all over the world, they know what they're doing!

Obviously – and this is the case for any solving solution – you must be familiar with the parts of the Rubik's Cube and their labels before you start. The only other prerequisite is to also know the algorithm terminology (see page 78), so you can easily follow the simple instructions for solving any Rubik's Cube.

The beginner's method solve is undertaken layer by layer, in a slower and more simple manner than, say, the CFOP method (see page 40 for details – when you are comfortable enough to move on to your next big solving challenge).

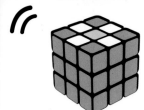

1. Create a 'daisy' (white cross around a yellow centre).

2. White cross with matching edges and centre pieces.

3. White face (with matching edges, corners and centre pieces).

4. Turn over, then get middle layer edges in place.

5. Yellow cross on top face.

6. Complete the yellow face.

7. Top face corners correctly positioned.

8. Edges in place: Finished!

YOU DID IT!

The available resources for this solving method are almost countless, from the official rubiks.com site to hundreds of online videos, so keep looking for the explanation that suits you. Eventually you will find the right description, and then the fun – and solving satisfaction – can start.

If someone you know shows you how to solve a Rubik's Cube, chances are they will show you this method, largely because it features a relatively small number of algorithms to learn. When you are more comfortable and familiar with them you can move on to the more 'serious' learning methods, but you will have a whole lot more to learn in terms of pattern recognition and algorithms. The pay-off is seriously low solving times!

THE FIRST EVER CUBE SOLVE

12

Professor Rubik constructed his first working cube out of wooden blocks in 1974, which was held together with elastic and paper clips.

At that point it was not clear that he had created a puzzle (he thought of it as art), and he later admitted that he did not even know if it was solvable!

So, how do you learn to solve a Rubik's Cube these days? Probably from a helpful Rubik's guide, a video or a book. Maybe with an app, or perhaps you learned from an interactive Cube that helped you along the way – perhaps a friend taught you. Well, just imagine if you had nobody to tell you how to get your Cube back in order? That's what Ernő Rubik was faced with back then. And although the Cube was his very own creation, the first wooden prototype was not decorated with the colours that give us the visual clues that

⬆ A very early photo of Professor Rubik, dating from around the mid-1970s.

we are so familiar with today. It was, of course, marked, but there were no easy-to-follow algorithms we take for granted. Professor Rubik only had a pen and paper to help him – not even the most basic home computer.

So, the story goes, it took Rubik around one month to solve the very first Cube for the very first time: that demonstrates perseverance! Many people would have given up by then and moved on to something simpler – or just taken it to pieces and put it back together in the right order (a popular, almost credible, solving technique in the 1980s).

Fortunately for us, Rubik was a man who relished the challenge and he continued turning, twisting and manipulating his prototype until it was back as it was when he started. And then he did it again, and took steps to get it out to the world.

'The moment I started twisting the sides, I could see it was a proper puzzle – but what I didn't know was whether it could be solved. It took me weeks.'
Professor Rubik, 2015

SPEED CUBERS ON SCREEN

13

The world of serious speedcubing – where competitors take part in multiple competitions that usually culminate in a World Championship title run – can seem distant, lonely and mysterious.

The Speed Cubers, a film directed by Sue Kim in 2020, offers a rather unexpected insight into that world. Following the lives of top cubers Feliks Zemdegs and Max Park in the run-up to the 2019 World Cube Association's World Championships in Melbourne, Australia, this Oscar-nominated documentary is a touching film that focuses on the human side of competition rather than the numbers. We learn of Max Park's autism diagnosis, his discovery

> **'Max is the king . . . He's just the best at everything.'**
>
> **Feliks Zemdegs**

of the Cube and how it helps his condition. At the time Max was the young pretender, hoping to dislodge the champion Zemdegs. The pair became – and remain – firm friends.

The movie provides great insight into the humanity and respect that can exist between competitors.

A NETFLIX ORIGINAL DOCUMENTARY

THE SPEED CUBERS

SOLVING:

14

**CFOP is not a new pop band or a company –
it's a fast method of solving the Rubik's Cube.**

It is also known as the Fridrich method, after the pioneering speedcuber Jessica Fridrich. Her method gained popularity in the late twentieth century, although many of the algorithms had been in use since the 1980s.

Fridrich was a prominent speedcuber in the early days of the sport, and she won the Czechoslovak championship in 1982 – a remarkable feat considering she had only seen a Rubik's Cube for the first time one year earlier. Her win secured an invitation to attend the first Rubik's Cube World Championship in Budapest later that year, where she placed tenth with a best time of 29.11 seconds.

Unlike the standard beginner's method (see page 48), CFOP starts with a cross on one side (traditionally white) and builds up the first two layers before the cube is completed. The precise steps are as follows:

1. **C**ross
2. **F**irst two layers (F2L)
3. **O**rient last layer (OLL)
4. **P**ermute last layer (PLL)

Casual cubers may be interested (and possibly a little bit frightened) to learn that there are 78 algorithms to

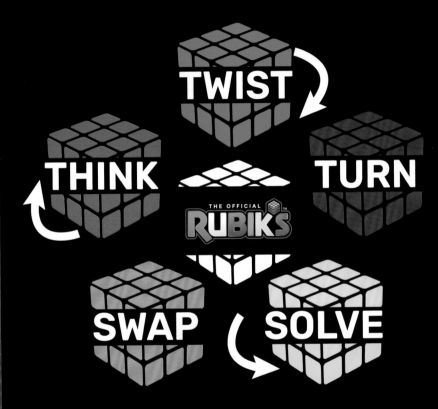

TWIST

TURN

THINK

THE OFFICIAL
RUBIK'S

SWAP

SOLVE

learn in order to master this method. However, if you want to get serious about your speedcubing and get your times down to single digits, this is certainly one way to do so.

The most successful speedcubers of the modern era, including Max Park and Feliks Zemdegs, use this method. It is acknowledged to be less intuitive than other methods, relying on numerous algorithms and careful pattern recognition, but the results speak for themselves.

It should be said that this method is only for those who want an extra level of challenge from their cubing.

Most solvers are more than happy to puzzle away, make patterns and show their peers, parents and carers the magic of a solved cube regardless of how long it takes!

Unsolved (scrambled) Cube.

1. Cross: The four edge pieces around one centre are solved first, making the cross shape on the bottom of the cube.

2. F2L: The four corners are solved at the same time, filling in the cross.

3. OLL: The top layer is filled in with the correct colour, although not necessarily in the correct places.

4. PLL: Top layer pieces are moved to their correct locations.

LUBRICATION: SPEEDING UP YOUR CUBE

15

If you thought solving a cube at the highest level is only about spinning it quickly, think again.

There is an entire industry dedicated to improving your solving speed. But for now, forget *how* to do it – solving a cube is a given when you get to this level in your Rubik's Cube journey.

One of the most important physical benefits a cube can have is lubrication. Pretty much every serious speedcuber uses one method or another to shave milliseconds off their solving times.

The principle of lubrication is simple and is the same for any other friction issue: applying lubrication to a factory-made cube will enable faster turns, quicker twists and smarter moves. When you've applied lube, you should notice faster solving times pretty much straight away.

Not all lubrication is the same: there are silicone oils, shock oils and differential oils available commercially, and many recipes for home-made variants.

➡ Make sure you do not apply too much lube to your cube!

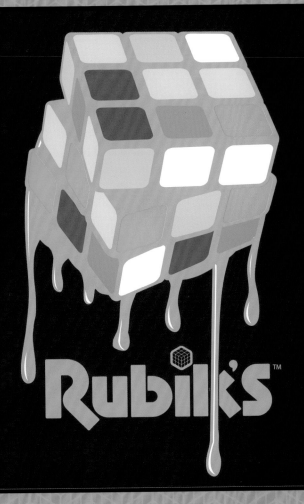

VARIATIONS ON A THEME...

#16

As we know, the first cube that Professor Rubik developed was 3x3, but once that one had hit the market and become a global bestseller and obsession, the professor turned his attention to other sizes.

There are now Rubik's Cubes that are 2x2, 4x4 and 5x5, usually with the familiar colour coding of the original 3x3 Cube from the 1970s.

The 4x4 Cube, originally titled 'Rubik's Revenge', is the next step up in the Rubik's series. It is made up of fifty-six cubies and the mechanical functions are very similar to the original, with the addition of some extra moves while solving (multiple 'sides' can be moved at once).

◆– A Rubik's keyring Cube and a 2x2 Rubik's Cube.

➡ Rubik's Blocks offers 3x3 fans a fresh challenge.

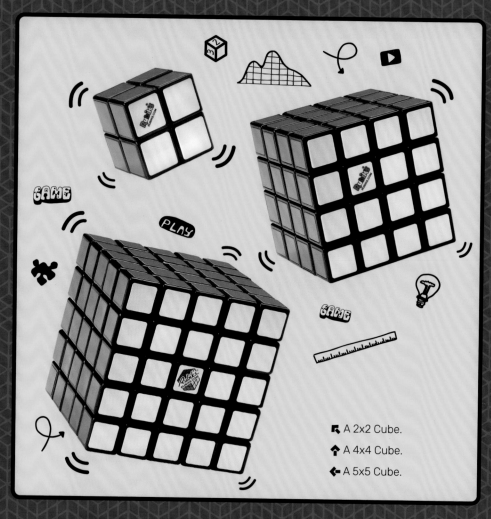

↖ A 2x2 Cube.
↑ A 4x4 Cube.
← A 5x5 Cube.

Mathematics fans out there will be impressed to know that the 4x4 has 7.4 quattuordecillion combinations (no, I'd never heard that term before either). This does cause a significant increase in solving times, with the record in 2024 at just under 16 seconds (Max Park, since you ask).

The 5x5 Cube takes it up another notch, as you would imagine. The 5x5 has twenty-five tiles per side and offers yet another stiff challenge to even the most experienced cube solver. This time, the number of combinations has increased to 282, 870,942,277,741,856,536,180,333,107, 150, 328, 293, 127, 731, 985, 672, 134, 721, 536,000,000, 000,000,000 – a vast number.

Again, this Rubik's Cube can be solved with (fairly) simple instruction and algorithms, but it is probably a good idea to be very familiar with the 3x3 Rubik's Cube and the 4x4 first.

You might think that a small Cube has a small number of permutations, but unfortunately, you'd be wrong. The 2x2 Rubik's Cube – the smallest in the series – still has more than 3.6 million possible variations. That's a lot less than a 3x3, but it's still a significant number of combos – instructions or demonstrations will be required!

Another that's not quite like the others is the Rubik's Block. Looking like an impressive optical illusion, this variation on a familiar theme offers a whole new challenge to cube solvers everywhere. The colours are the same as on the 3x3 Rubik's Cube, but this time the shape can vary with each turn, making for a very different feel from the puzzle. To solve this one, you have to re-create the shape as well as align the colours.

With all these Cube variations, there is an almost endless possibility for fun challenges and puzzle solving!

CUBE SOUNDS

#17

Here we look at the cube in music, where it appears frequently, usually as an interesting feature in performance or video.

A special shout goes out to **Harry Styles**, the former One Direction megastar, as his global tour featured a Rubik's Cube displayed in the opening animation before every concert.

Rubik's Cubes have appeared in many music videos over the years; here are a few – look out for others!

• Back in 1986, **Genesis** included one in a music video for the song 'Land of Confusion'. It is being solved by a Spock-alike puppet

• Fast forward to 1998, and one of the most famous appearances of a Rubik's Cube in a video: the **Spice Girls**' number one hit, 'Viva Forever'.

• The Rubik's Cube is central to **Magic Box**'s video for the 2003 song 'If You . . . '. The colour palette and shapes are a central part of the video.

• The Rubik's Cube appears in **Jennifer Lopez**'s 'Ain't Your Mama' video, made to accompany her 2016 single.

• **Taylor Swift** – who wasn't born when the Rubik's Cube came out – has one in her video for the 2017 song 'End Game', featuring **Ed Sheeran** and **Future**, in a sequence littered with nostalgic 1980s items.

➡ Images from the Harry Styles tour of 2018. What was he trying to say?

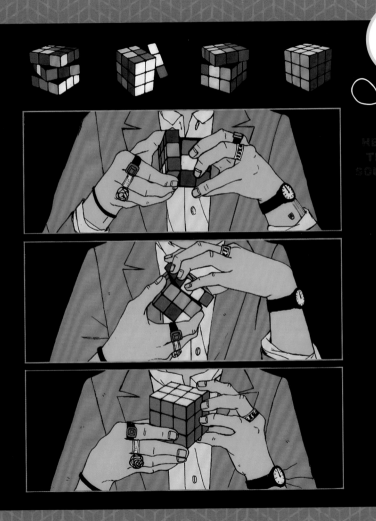

HEAR
THE
SOUND!

59

SOLVING: ROUX   #18

The Roux method of solving the Rubik's Cube is one of the most popular for speedcubers, after the CFOP method. However, it has been gaining popularity of late, with a few more podium finishes in big competitions than previously.

As we saw with the CFOP method (see page 40), this is for cubers who have mastered the basics of solving the Rubik's Cube and are looking to get into some serious competition and blistering times. Having said that, there's no reason why any serious Rubik's Cube fan should not have a go at mastering some of the complicated aspects of this endlessly fascinating puzzle.

The Roux method was created by French speedcuber Gilles Roux, who used it to good effect in the first decade of the twenty-first century. His legacy has endured, and there are many online tutorials and videos online, demonstrating the popularity of the method.

There are four main sequences.

Start with a scrambled cube.

1. First Block (a 1x2x3 section is solved).

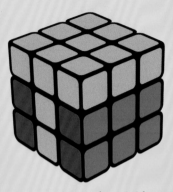

2. Second Block (a matching block on the opposite side).

3. CMLL (Corners of the Last Layer).

4. Last Six Edges (also known as L6E).

COMPUTER SOLVING POWER

19

When the Rubik's Cube was first released and was spinning and twisting its way to global popularity, another phenomenon was taking place: the home computing revolution.

With a trajectory that almost matches the Rubik's Cube's own, the home computer first became popular throughout the 1980s, and by the time the Sinclair ZX81 had been released, the computer had transformed from something in a science fiction novel to a reality on your kitchen table.

However, it was to be a few years before the computer would be useful for solving the Rubik's Cube. Fast forward to the twenty-first century and dedicating solving robots are able to solve a fully scrambled cube in less than half of one second.

Computers are specifically designed to recognize patterns and can store hundreds of long (or short) algorithms that relate to them. So once technology existed for the accurate visual scanning of a cube, the analysis of the layout and storing and enacting of algorithms, and once the mechanics to enact them had been developed, it was only a matter of time before robots started to make their way into the fastest solving lists.

SOLVING

IN PROGRESS

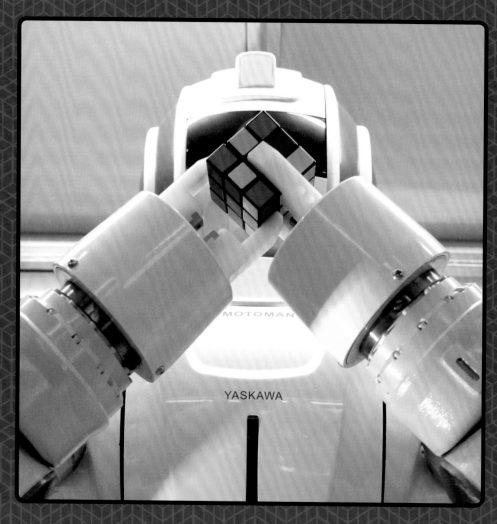

One huge breakthrough (sub one-second) came from the Sub 1 robot, which for a time held the Guinness World Record for a robot solve of the cube. That was broken and, as of 2024, it is 0.38 seconds, held by a custom-built computer made by MIT students Ben Katz and Jared Di Carlo.

It has been observed that a human can perform around ten or twelve turns of a cube per second. A robot is able to make more than fifty in that same time frame, giving the machine a huge advantage. The robot's ability to halt a turn to within a few millimetres provides another distinct advantage – there's no 'catching' of an edge for a robot. Couple that with the programming and memory-access technology and it is no surprise that machines are able to out-think humans when cubing.

However, the difference between man and machine is only around two seconds, so hardly a huge gap. It will be a long time before humans can do a sub-one-second solve, but watch out: when a 22-second solve was the record, a completion time of less than five seconds was thought to be out of this world. The rate at which technology advances is clearly demonstrated by the robot solving record's progression from 2010, when it was 50 seconds, to today's blink of an eye!

← A cube-solving robot from the Macau Science Center.

↑ The Cubestormer II – made of Lego parts and running on Android, 2011.

CUBE
CHAMPS

20

Millions of people have owned, played with and solved the Rubik's Cube over the years. Some have gone on to compete, pitting their skills against the best in the world. A few have become champions, broken records and even changed the way the cube is solved. Here are just a few of the characters involved in speedcubing . . .

Max Park

Max (born 2001) has become a legendary Cube solver in just a few years, and he can definitely be regarded as one of the all-time legends. He's from California in the USA and by 2024 Max had broken the Single and Average World Records for the 3x3, 4x4, 5x5, 6x6 and 7x7 cubes. Oh, and he holds the one-handed 3x3 solving record too. Knowing Max, you can be sure he'll be trying his hardest to beat them all!

Minh Thai

Minh Thai, born in 1965, will be forever famous as the winner of the very first Rubik's Cube World Championship. He travelled to Budapest in 1982 following his win at the US Championships the year before. At the time he was a sixteen-year-old student and his winning time of 22.95 seconds on a 3x3 cube stood for twenty years – until 2003.

Feliks Zemdegs

Only two cubers to date have won the world championships twice: Max Park and Feliks Zemdegs. Born in Melbourne, Australia, in 1995, Feliks got his first cube in 2008 and set his first cubing world record by January 2010. He dominated the speedcubing scene for the next decade, winning two world championships and breaking records consistently.

Jessica Fridrich

This speedcuber was so influential she gave her name to an entire solving technique! Fridrich was one of the original cubing generation, starting not long after the Cube came out. Hailing from Czechoslovakia, Fridrich triumphed in her national championships and earned a place at the world championships in 1982, where she came tenth.

Erik Akkersdijk

Erik is a Dutch speedcuber who has held many national records, and – notably – was the world record holder for the 3x3 cube (7.08 seconds) until Feliks Zemdegs arrived on the scene and took over the mantle. Erik has contributed much to the world of cube solving, and has held more than thirty world records at various times during his fascinating cubing career.

Yu Nakajima (中島悠)

Yu, from Hokkaido, Japan, is a speed solver who held world records between 2008 and 2012, including the fastest time for a 3x3 solve and the 5x5 (54.86 seconds). He was also the Rubik's Cube World Champion in 2007, and has contributed significantly to the evolution of the sport of speedcubing.

'Not in my wildest dreams I would ever imagine that someone could solve the cube this fast.'

Jessica Fridrich on Feliks Zemdegs, 2012

'Speedcubing is a magical glue that holds a global cubing community together.'

Professor Rubik, 2021

CUBE MAGIC! #21

Rubik's Cubes have long been associated with intelligence and are often used as a symbol of being smart. Another place they are regularly seen is in the hands of magicians. Possibly the most famous is Steven Brundage, who notably appeared on the *Fool Us* television show hosted by Penn and Teller. It was not Brundage's first brush with popularity – he once performed a cube trick for some police officers who had pulled him over in his car. Brundage took a scrambled cube, moved it behind his back, threw it over his shoulder and it landed in his hand fully solved; the video was an internet sensation.

His amazing tricks for Penn and Teller included placing a scrambled cube in a bag and removing it completed, breathing on a cube to solve it and the amazing back throw. He has also wowed audiences on *America's Got Talent* and more.

Another cube magician is Paul Vu, who performed a seemingly instant cube solve while burning a napkin, and transformed a mini-cube into a pile of M&Ms! In another trick he drew a picture of host Ellen DeGeneres on the separate white parts of a cube before assembling them for a fully formed cartoon image. On that show, he used a random pile of cubes to make an image of the subject DeGeneres was thinking of – Super Mario. It was a stunning trick that involved mind reading, cube manipulation and cube mosaic art.

1. An early example (1982) of a Rubik's Cube trick on television: Austrian Peter Lodynski was an actor, performer and magician who featured a cube in his magic act not long after its release.

2. Japanese magician Cyril performs a cube trick at a reception for the Rubik's Cube fortieth anniversary in Tokyo, 2020.
3. Magician Steven Brundage regularly performs cube tricks.

CUBEVOLUTION! #22

From a stiff wooden prototype to a smooth spinning mechanism, the Rubik's Cube has evolved plenty over the years. But the fundamentals remain the same . . .

As we've seen, Rubik's first Cube was a long way from the production model. In fact, most of today's fans would not even recognize the original as being the granddaddy of the Rubik's Cube. Even the standard Rubik's Cube available today has a slick movement not present in the earliest models, and there are now many variations of the 3x3 Rubik's Cube, alongside other models.

If you get hold of an original Rubik's Cube today, you will probably be surprised by how stiff it is (not just because it is fifty years old). Rubik's Cubes made today are generally faster and less stiff in comparison, and when you get on to specifically constructed, fast cubes such as the Rubik's Speed model, there is a hugely noticeable difference.

Let's look at just a few of the various Rubik's Cubes that have been available throughout the years . . .

The original 'Magic Cube' was first released in the 1970s and came packaged in a small cardboard box. The colours are just as we know them today, and of course the size, shape and method of manipulation has not changed at all. There have been

73

10

11

12

13

14

many different 3x3 Rubik's Cubes released, including a few special editions for various anniversaries: 30th (wooden), 40th and 50th (gold face). Other releases have been to help with solving (Tutor Cube/Coach Cube), speed (Rubik's Speed), both (Rubik's Connected) or different puzzle elements (Rubik's Impossible, Rubik's Crystal).

Currently, there's even a Rubik's Cube made from recycled plastic (Rubik's Re-Cube), and the useful 'perpetual' Rubik's Calendar that lets you display the date differently every day of the year; these were produced with different language options as the calendar is text-based.

There are also editions of the Rubik's Cube with special colour palettes, including the Rubik's Icon (monochrome – see Wednesday Adams) and the Texture model limited edition, which is all black with sides of different textures. As part of their retro series, Rubik's released a special Hungarian Cube complete with the first name of the Cube: *Bűvös Kocka*.

Lately, the *Stranger Things* Rubik's Cube, the Disney Theme Park 50th Anniversary and the Disney 100th Anniversary Cubes have proved themselves very popular.

1. Professor Rubik's early prototype (*c.*1975) **2.** 'Magic Cube' (1980) **3.** Rubik's Cube (1981) **4.** Rubik's Cube Calendar (1981) **5.** 30th Anniversary wooden Cube (2010) **6.** Rubik's Icon (*c.*2010) **7.** Rubik's Phantom Cube (2022) **8.** Rubik's Coach Cube (2023) **9.** Rubik's 3x3 Classic Cube (2023) **10.** Rubik's Impossible Cube (2023) **11.** Rubik's Cube *Stranger Things* (2023) **12.** Rubik's Cube *Wednesday* (2023) **13.** Rubik's Aeon Black Texture Cube (special edition, Japan, 2023) **14.** Rubik's Crystal Cube (2024).

BOOKS ABOUT THE CUBE

23

All Rubik's Cubes come with instructions, but they were not always easy to follow for new adopters of the puzzle. It was not long before other solutions to solving became available.

It is worth remembering that this was pre-internet, pre-social media and before information could easily be shared electronically. Back in the twentieth century, if you wanted to learn more about a subject you would probably start in a library, or check a specialist magazine. If the subject was in the news, you might look in a newspaper.

In 1981, an English schoolboy named Patrick Bossert developed a method for solving the Rubik's Cube. After taking it to pieces and reassembling it, he noticed that the centre pieces were connected ('and that's when the penny dropped. I now knew that I was able to solve it').

He wrote his method down, added diagrams and reproduced it, selling copies to school friends. This was noticed by an executive who worked for a publishing company, and the decision was made to adapt his system into a full book, entitled *You Can Do the Cube*. It was released in England and became an instant bestseller; it was then published in many other countries around the world. In October 1981, the book hit the number one spot on *The New York Times Bestseller* list, and at thirteen, Patrick became the youngest author ever to top that list. His book reportedly sold more than 1.5 million copies worldwide.

1. First published in the USA, James Nourse's Cube instruction book sold millions of copies.

2. Bossert's 1981 solving method appeared in the book *You Can Do the Cube*, published by Puffin, a children's book imprint.

3. Hungary's *Ezermester* ('Handyman') magazine from August 1977 featured an illustrated solution to the 'Magic Cube'.

CUBE
NOTATION

#24

When you are learning to solve the Rubik's Cube it will help if you can understand the instructions easily. Fortunately, after fifty years, the world has settled on a series of universals.

As the diagrams opposite demonstrate, each part of a Rubik's Cube has a name, and each section too, in order for everyone to understand and share knowledge related to it. Edges, corners, faces – all these will probably be familiar to you by now, but if not, here is a great opportunity to learn.

As you graduate to more complicated solving methods you will need to learn the advanced notation too, and if you decide to learn 4x4 or 5x5 cubes, they have some of their own special terms and (multi-part) moves.

When used as part of an algorithm, the letters refer to a quarter turn of that cube's face, so when you see U it means a clockwise quarter turn of the upper face; and an apostrophe and U' means an anti-clockwise turn of the upper face, and so on.

Algorithms are essential elements when it comes to learning how to solve a cube efficiently and are used for solving, scrambling as well as pattern-making (see page 88).

CUBE ELEMENTS

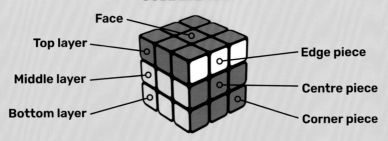

Face

Top layer

Middle layer

Bottom layer

Edge piece

Centre piece

Corner piece

TURNS

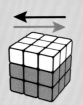

Up face = U
Reverse = U'

Left face = L
Reverse = L'

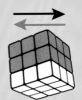

Down face = D
Reverse = D'

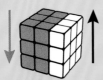

Right face = R
Reverse = R'

Front = F
Reverse = F'

Back = B
Reverse = B'

OTHER RUBIK CREATIONS

25

As you would imagine, Professor Rubik did not stop after creating the 3x3 Rubik's Cube. Here are some of his other 3D puzzle creations.

Rubik's Snake

Developing a fidget toy before the world even knew what a fidget toy was, Professor Rubik showed great vision once again with the development of the Snake. Twenty-four wedges were joined together in such a way that they can be twisted but not separated.

This meant that a wide variety of shapes could be formed, with many creative possibilities. The Snake hit the shelves in 1981, not long after the Cube, and it is still popular today, enjoying a resurgence as a fidget toy. A similar shape-shifting puzzle is the Rubik's Twist, which comes in the classic Cube colours.

Rubik's Magic

This puzzle toy (right) was released in 1986, and it is a cleverly interlinking series of eight square tiles with patterns that are held together by flexible wires that allow them to be rearranged in different ways. The puzzle can be folded flat or 'stacked' and a loop can be formed as well. It is a fascinating, highly original puzzle, and it still enjoys a cult following nearly four decades after its release. Despite the (relatively) low number of variations possible compared to the Cube, Rubik's Magic still offers a significant intellectual challenge to twisty puzzle fans of all ages.

Upon release, the Magic was also very popular all over the world – competitions were staged and solving records were set.

A slightly different version was also released, the Rubik's Magic: Master Edition.

COLOSSAL
CUBES

26

Not all working cubes are sized the same – some are huge!

At one point, the largest functioning Rubik's Cube ever – according to the *Guinness Book of Records* – was in the Nina Mall, Hong Kong, China, in 2021 (opposite).

This vast Rubik's Cube was around 2.5 metres (8 ft) across, but it was unlikely that anyone would break any solving records with it – it took three people to move each side one turn! It was constructed on site by a team of specialists, and the colour stickers were added at the end once the whole mechanism was in place.

But in December 2023, in the Dubai Knowledge Park, a new cube was crowned as the largest ever. This one measured a vast 3 metres (9¾ ft) each side and was made of fibreglass.

One previous record holder was puzzle master Tony Fisher, whose big cube was constructed in Ipswich in the UK in 2019. It measured 2.022 metres (6 ft 7 in.) across, but didn't have the record for long, for it was bettered (biggered?) in Calgary, Canada, only two years later. Unveiled in the Telus Spark Science Center in Calgary, this cube was designed by Wes Nelson. How big will the next record holder be – and will it need a crane to turn it?

CUBE
SCULPTURES

There are some giant, working cubes out there. But not all large cubes have been built as functioning objects of mechanical wonder: some are just nice to look at.

27

Ernő Rubik himself is credited as the designer of a large steel-framed sculpture of a huge Rubik's Cube. In fact, it is a cube within a cube, the central one solid and the surrounding one a steel frame with empty cuboids. This impressive monument was created by Hungarian sculptor Róbert Németh and was unveiled in 2010. It is located in Budapest, alongside various other sculptures.

Also in Hungary, in the town of Százhalombatta, is a giant cube sculpture. This one is made of plastic and glass, but it also features more than one thousand solar-powered lights that come on automatically after dark. Unveiled in 2004, it was the work of three designers.

In Odessa, Ukraine, there is a large Rubik's Cube sculpture on a stand.

1. Xi'an flower exposition, China.

2. Gorky Park, Odessa, Ukraine.

3. South Bank, London.

4. SM Seaside City, Sebu, Philippines.

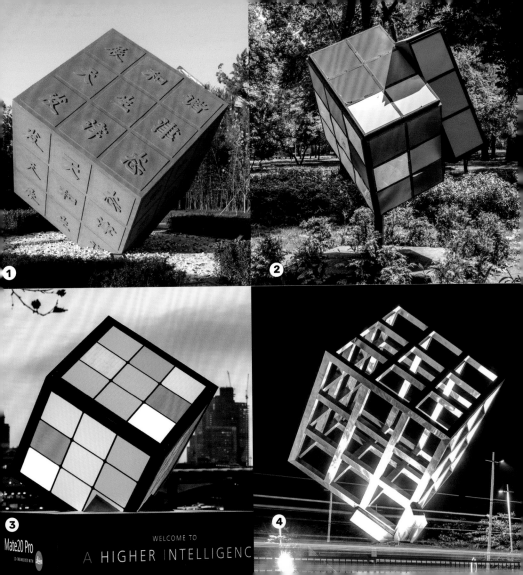

It is in the city's Gorky Park, which was well known as the location of a famous novel with the same name by Martin Cruz Smith. The book was first published in 1981 – the year the Cube gained global popularity.

Also in Europe, Belgium's Liège railway station featured a cube atop its stunning modern design for one year, and later a series of coloured filters were placed over the station's structure, making it look like a huge, spread-out cube. The Gare de Liège-Guillemins was designed by Spanish architect Santiago Calatrava, and the artwork, by French artist Daniel Buren, was called *Comme tombées du ciel, les couleurs in situ et en mouvement* ('as if fallen from the sky, colours in place and moving'). It lit up beautifully internally and externally.

Further afield, there is a large cubic sculpture in Zabeel Park, Dubai, which was opened in 2005. It is an 8x8(!) cube, so is predominantly chess-oriented, but it does make you wonder if you could reach out and turn it. Made of stainless steel and copper, it was created by sculptor David Harber.

And in New York's Astor Place, Manhattan, the Astor Place cube is a popular sculpture. Resembling a 2x2 Cube, it can be rotated, but it is not fully mechanical so cannot be 'solved.' It has, however, been decorated to resemble a Rubik's Cube on occasion. 'Alamo', by the artist Tony Rosenthal, has been in this location since 1967, predating the Rubik's Cube.

1. and **2.** Steel sculpture in the Graphisoft Park, Budapest.

3. 'Alamo', Astor Place Cube, New York City, USA.

4. Sculpture by Tamás Sándor, Márta Fischer, István Varga, Százhalombatta Hungary.

PATTERNS

#28

When solving a cube, the object is to get it back into its perfect state, with all sides complete. But there are many pretty patterns you can make on a cube . . .

When you start out with a nice, neat, complete Rubik's Cube, your first desire is to keep it perfect. But if you want to solve it, you first have to scramble it.

However, Rubik's Cube patterns are a creative way of playing with a cube and all can be made by following simple algorithms. Some are famous: 'Cube in a Cube' and 'Cube in a Cube in a Cube', and the 'Easy Chessboard' is one you can probably figure out for yourself. But there are a few that when you start to study them you realize they must

have some serious twisting action behind them. Here are a few of our favourites, along with the algorithms to make them (see page 78 for details on the notation).

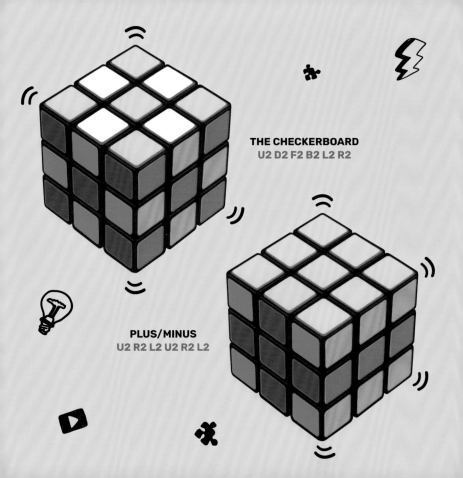

THE CHECKERBOARD
U2 D2 F2 B2 L2 R2

PLUS/MINUS
U2 R2 L2 U2 R2 L2

LINES
R2 U2 R2 U2 R2 U2 L2 D2 L2
D2 L2 D2 L2 R2

SIDE LINES
R D R F R F' F' B D R' U' B' U D2

SUPERFLIP
U R2 F B R B2 R U2 L B2 R U'
D' R2 F R' L B2 U2 F2

CUBE IN A CUBE
F L F U' R U F2 L2 U' L' B
D' B' L2 U

CUBE IN A CUBE IN A CUBE
U' L' U' F' R2 B' R F U B2 U B' L U' F U R F'

CHESSBOARD IN A CUBE
B D F' B' D L2 U L U' B D' R B R
D' R L' F U2 D

CENTRES
U D' R L' F B' U D'

OPPOSITE CORNERS
R L U2 F2 D2 F2 R L F2 D2 B2 D2

VERTICAL STRIPES
F U F R L2 B D' R D2 L D' B R2 L F U F

SHIFTED BLOCKS
L2 B2 D' B2 D L2 U R2 D R2 B
U R' F2 R U' B' U'

HELLO!
U2 R2 F2 U2 D2 F2 L2 U2

40 (4T)
F2 D2 F' L2 D2 U2 R2 B' U2 F2

COLOURS #29

**What's in a colour? If you asked an artist,
you'd probably get a very long answer.
And the Cube's colours are very important . . .**

The first Rubik Cubes were produced using the colour palette that we know so well – the colours were chosen by Rubik for his original design, before the Cube was even a puzzle! There was a later variation, known as the 'Japanese' colour palette, because of its popularity there. It had blue next to green and opposite white.

This was a deviation from the original colours, also known as BOY (Blue-Orange-Yellow) or the 'western' colour palette. Even now, there are a few speedcubers who prefer to use cubes with that different colour palette, but they are certainly in a tiny minority. Professor Rubik said: 'I decided to decorate the surface of each of the six sides of the cube. From the sheer unlimited number of possibilities for the types and designs of surface decorations and markings (dots, crosses and all other graphic symbols, numbers, letters, colors etc.), I finally decided on solid, uniformly coloured surfaces. I specifically chose six bright colours that were not too close to each other and that look delightful to me.'

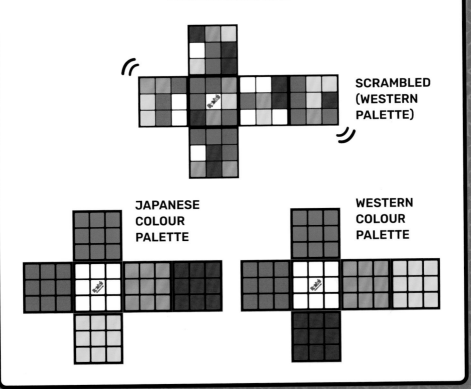

'I needed some sort of coding to bring sense to the rotations of the cube, so I used the simplest and strongest solution: primary colours.'

Professor Rubik, 2015

SCRAMBLED (WESTERN PALETTE)

JAPANESE COLOUR PALETTE

WESTERN COLOUR PALETTE

VOCABULARY

#30

Rubik's Cubes have their own vocabulary; here's a basic list . . .

Algorithm – A set series of moves that are used to manipulate the pieces on a cube, to solve it or make a pattern.

Beginner's Method – The most simple method for solving a cube.

Buttery – A super smooth turning cube.

CFOP – A solving method, one of the most commonly used methods by speedcubers.

Centre – The middle pieces on a cube's face.

Corner cutting – When speedcubing, this refers to making a new turn even with a slight misalignment in another face.

Cubie – Small, individual cubes that make up a cube.

DNF – Did not finish. Refers to a cube solve gone wrong (in a competition).

DNS – Did not start. This is when a solve is not even attempted (in a competition).

Devil's Algorithm – A (very long!) algorithm that takes the cube through every possible combination of configurations.

F2L – First two layers.

FMC – Fewest move count; a competitive category where the winner solves the cube with the fewest number of moves.

Finger tricks – Special moves a cuber employs while solving.

God's Algorithm – The shortest possible algorithm for solving a cube.

Gummy – Term for a cube that has components that do not turn very quickly.

Half turn – A 180-degree turn of a cube. (Most notation refers to quarter turns.)

Layer – One of the cube's constituent parts. There are thee layers: top, centre and bottom.

Lube – Lubrication to make your cube twist faster.

Mod – Any 'modification' you make to a cube.

Move Count – The number of moves you use to solve a cube.

Notation – A standard form for communicating which moves to make when solving.

OH – One-handed.

Picture Cube – A Rubik's Cube with images on the faces instead of colours.

Prime – Part of notation, indicating an anti-clockwise move.

Quarter turn – One turn of a cube's face (90 degrees).

Roux – A solving method developed by Gilles Roux.

Slice – A move involving moving the central column or row of your cube (or two opposite sides, depending on how you look at it).

Scrambled – a mixed-up cube.

Sticker – Peeling them off and sticking back on was a common occurrence for non-solvers.

TPS – Turns per second: more is better as long as they are accurate!

WCA – World Cube Association

ZZ – A solving method (named after Zbigniew Zborowski, its creator).

EXERCISE
PREPARATION

31

If you are a sensible person and you want to stay healthy, you would not sprint a race or compete in a match without a proper warm-up – and it is no different when it comes to cubing.

Warming up before any exercise is important, and cubing is no exception. True, you may not need to skip for a while or do some press-ups and calf stretches, but a few finger exercises will ensure you start your session with your digits in the very best condition possible, and that can only be a good thing.

Remember to try these very gently at first, and stop immediately if you feel any pain or resistance: these are designed to be simple, light warm-up exercises only.

Shake it off: keeping your fingers relaxed, shake your wrists out gently, both at the same time.

Wrist roll: link your fingers and roll your wrists around in an easy, loose fashion.

Flick out: flick all of your fingers on both hands out at the same time.

Finger pull: gently stretch each finger by wrapping the fingers of the other hand around it and pulling very gently.

Make fists: make gentle fists, then open out your fingers and stretch them out, keeping them next to each other. Repeat a four or five times.

Namaste: place your palms together in front of your chest and apply gentle pressure to stretch the wrists very gently.

IMPOSSIBLE! #32

When you see a scrambled Rubik's Cube (in real life or on screen) you automatically assume that it is solvable. After all, that is the whole point, isn't it?

However, the Rubik's Cube is constrained by the laws of mechanics, physics and mathematics, which means that you may see a Rubik's Cube that is actually impossible to solve. There may be various reasons for this, but the most common is – unfortunately – that someone took it apart and didn't put it back together properly! Many people do not realize that the Rubik's Cube is a precision instrument and that despite 43 quintillion combinations, there are some that are impossible.

The other most common cause is mis-stickering: someone was not paying attention or – even worse – thought it would be fun to offer a friend the ultimate problem cube (see *The Big Bang Theory*).

Fortunately, there are ways to spot impossible scrambles . . . Without diving into the heavy mathematics of factorials, permutations and symmetric groups, here is what to look out for on an 'unsolvable' Rubik's Cube:

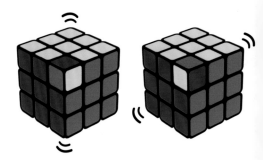

It is impossible to have a single twisted corner on a solvable cube.

 Edge pieces cannot be simply swapped, either adjacently or opposite each other.

Opposite corner pieces cannot be simply swapped, either adjacently or opposite each other.

 Two centres cannot have the same colour.

Corners must each have three different colours.

 It is not possible to have one single incorrect edge.

STEM AND LEARNING

33

STEM stands for science, technology, engineering and mathematics – it's usually used in the context of education. Let's see how good solving is for you and your brain.

Science: learning about enquiring, problem-solving and research are all useful, if not essential parts of using a Rubik's Cube.

Technology: even without learning the history of the Rubik's Cube (see page 10), the technology of the puzzle is fascinating for young and old, new adopters and even those who have been solving for years. It is a relatively simple device, but prior to Professor Rubik's creation, there was nothing like it in the realm of puzzles, or toys.

Engineering: these days the Rubik's Cube is precision made, with tiled colours and beautifully spinning parts. The original Cubes were a little more basic, but one fascinating fact about the Rubik's Cube is that the basic concepts and construction process has changed very little in the half century since it first appeared in shops.

Mathematics: as we have seen previously, mathematics plays an important part in the culture of the Rubik's Cube, and it has fascinated many mathematicians, from teachers

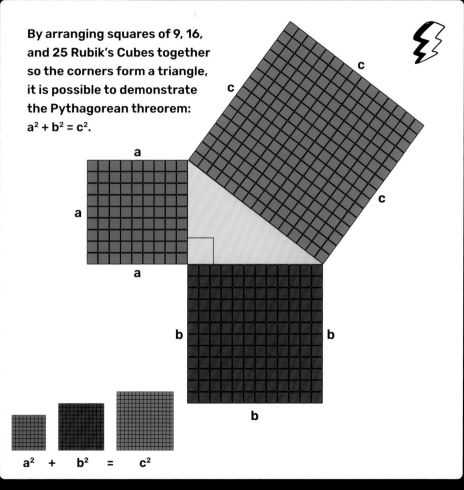

By arranging squares of 9, 16, and 25 Rubik's Cubes together so the corners form a triangle, it is possible to demonstrate the Pythagorean threorem: $a^2 + b^2 = c^2$.

c

c

c

c

a

a

a

a

b

b

b

b

a^2 + b^2 = c^2

in school classrooms to research professors in universities.

In fact, solving a Rubik's Cube can be a useful part of a discussion of geometry as it allows learners to study multiple procedures (algorithms). Symbols can be learned as part of this, in particular ones that may be completely new to the person learning.

The Rubik's Cube is really versatile in the educational context, and is frequently used in conjunction with learning other scientific principles, from manipulation of a cube (involving, say, giving and following simple instructions) to robot viewing, scanning and solving of a cube (highly advanced, with multiple complicated processes).

In the classroom, the Rubik's Cube can be used in a wide variety of ways to teach young (and older) people of all abilities. For example, fractions and ratios can be studied by looking at the number of different colour cuboids on various sides; for older students, the mathematics of solving the Cube can be a fascinating challenge (possible combinations!). And if you add more cubes, more principles can be demonstrated, for example, the Pythagorean theorem with groups of 9, 16 and 25 cubes (see diagram on previous page).

If you have enough cubes, they can even be used for learning about artistic matters, for example, how to make mosaics (and that could even touch on history). It seems like the learning possibilities are (almost) endless – similar to solving the Cube!

1. Schools Without Walls at the Marian Koshland Science Museum, 2010.

2. Primary school students with cubes, Australia, July 2010.

3. Cube-solving robot built during a Rubik's Camp event.

WCA REGULATIONS

34

Speedcubing is a serious business, and the rules and regulations must be carefully followed if you want to get on in a competitive environment. Here are a few to look out for.

The basics of cube competitions are straightforward: you turn up with your cube, you solve it a given number of times and then the results are announced. However:

• Remember to register for any competition well in advance.

• The cube you compete with must conform to the minimum regulations (these are readily available online from the WCA web site – see URL opposite). Make sure well in advance that your cube is competition legal!

• Once you are in the competition, timing is everything – assuming you make a clean solve. There are strict regulations for starting and stopping the timer, and these must be adhered to.

• Your puzzle will be scrambled, and you – naturally – have no say in this. It is done in complete secrecy.

• All the latest guidelines for events are available on the WCA's website: worldcubeassociation.org. It is worth checking out, to get an idea of what you are in for. Good luck!

1. Matty Hiroto, 3x3 event winner at the 2022 Rubik's WCA North American Championship.

2. Tyson and Toby Mao, brothers preparing to contest an event, 2005.

DIGITAL CUBE!   #35

Rubik's took a leap into the twenty-first century with the launch of the Rubik's Connected Cube . . .

One of the joys of the Rubik's Cube is that it exists in the moment, with no screens or diversions, no electricity needed, and nothing digital – until now.

However, the advantages of a Rubik's Connected are numerous and significant: there is help from a computer with every stage of learning and solving; perfect timing to the hundredth of a second; you can compete from the comfort of your armchair. And there is more. The clever Cube is even able to pair with your smartphone and can exchange data with its own app.

It has opened up a new world of instruction and competition, allowing cubers to track every solve and every time. The app features games to play, including a solving 'duel' where you connect to other cubers around the world and pit your wits (and your solving time) against them.

The Connected has been well received, and many serious (and not so serious) cubers use one for timing and learning, even if they do not use of all the competitive elements.

The Connected Cube could take your cubing to another level, with the help of modern technology.

107

CUBE BUILDINGS

We have seen solvable cubes big and small. We have seen giant cubes and sculptures in amazing places. Let's look at some cube-inspired buildings.

The first stop is in Australia, and the 'sunken cube' building in Melbourne. Part of the large Melbourne Museum site, the sunken cube houses the Children's Museum and is a colourful place. Although not really a cube, the bright colours and amazing design make you think of Rubik's original creation.

• Also in Australia, the d'Arenberg Cube is a building with an amazing distinctive geometric design, hugely reminiscent of a Rubik's Cube. The faces are mostly glass, and it is located in a wine-making district of South Australia, the owner of the vineyard, Chester Osborn, wanting an original building, explains, 'Wine is a bit of a puzzle with so many interconnected facets, so a Rubik's Cube is the perfect design to express that.' He certainly got it!

1. The Children's Museum, Melbourne.

2. The National Science Museum (Technopolis) in Bangkok, Thailand.

3. and **4.** The Play Country Building in Quan'an City, China (in and out).

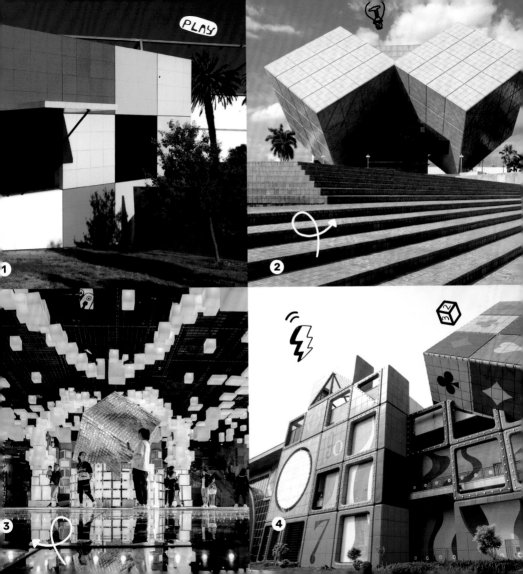

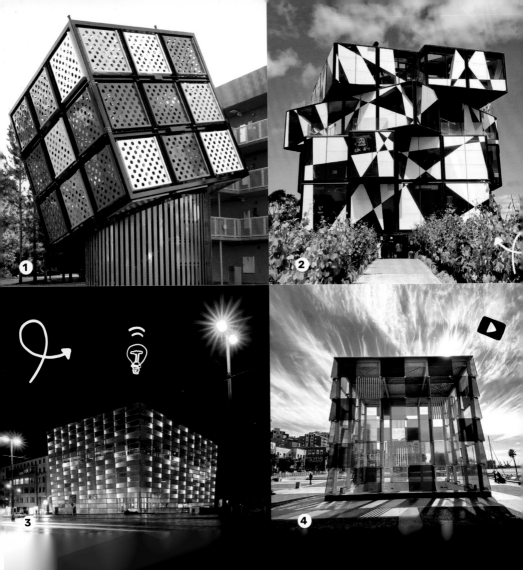

• China's Quan'an City boasts an extraordinary, colourful place known as the Rubik's Cube Play Country Building. It even has some stunning ('cubey') internal spaces.

• The National Science Museum (Technopolis) in Bangkok, Thailand, is another amazing looking building, resembling a series of joined cubes.

• London's Great Ormond Street Hospital has a colourful cube-styled element on the outside, forming a cover and extra floor space.

• In Austria, the glass front of the Ars Electronica building – a centre for electronic arts – in Linz was lit up like a Rubik's Cube. Using a specially adapted device, people could manipulate the cube and change the colours on the building. It was for a piece entitled Puzzle Façade by artist Javier Lloret, and even though it was only visible on two sides, the puzzle could still be solved.

• One building (the 1980s-themed, of course) in Disney's Pop Century Resort in Florida has a staircase that is an entire Rubik's Cube. Fortunately, it does not turn.

• In Spain, the Pompidou Centre in Málaga is a cubic building that has a very familiar colour scheme.

There are many more buildings all over the world that are reminiscent of Rubik's Cubes. Some are made like this deliberately, others coincidentally, but either way it serves to highlight the power of this special shape.

1. Disney Pop Century Resort, USA.
2. The d'Arenberg Cube, Australia.
3. Ars Electronica Center, Linz, Austria.
4. Pompidou Centre, Málaga, Spain.

CONSTRUCTION #37

The Rubik's Cube is made of plastic and metal, although you only see the former if all goes to plan.

After fifty years of use, practice and feedback, the Rubik's Cube is still largely the same now as it was back in the 1970s, but technological advancements mean more Cubes are produced to higher standards than ever before.

If you go back to an original Rubik's Cube, you would probably find it a bit stiff compared to today's models, and modern manufacturing means that Cubes that come off the production line today are the best they can be. The process is the same as it was half a century ago:

• Moulding: plastic parts are made by injection moulding.
• Assembly: the pre-constructed core has the cuboids grouped around it.
• Labelling/Tiling: depending on the cube type, either stickers or plastic tiles are added to the faces.
• Packaging: a cardboard box or a plastic blister pack.
• Quality Control: randomly tested at any point of the construction cycle. Then the cube is on its way to a shop near you.

➜ Workers assembling Rubik's Cubes in the factory in Budapest, around 1979.

EXTREME

38

Some people are not happy simply solving a Rubik's Cube. They like to take it bit further . . . Into the world of extreme cubing, where the impossible becomes possible!

Here are some of the (much) more extreme solving styles.

• Freefall: the golden rule for this type of extreme solving is don't drop the cube – it's a really long way down.

• Underwater solving: it is not the speed at which you can solve, it is the number of cubes you are able to solve while totally submerged under water and holding your breath.

• Other popular ones are the simultaneous solve of two cubes while upside down, the solve while running 100 metres (you may need to run a bit slower to succeed), hoverboard bicycle, unicycle and – most dangerously – motorbike.

We do not recommend any of these activities, but look out for the next extreme cubing attempt at a track/ pool/sky near you.

1. Pogo stick: Xia Yan from China, 2021.

2. Thomas Kohn, Germany, 2007.

3. Skydiving solve by entrepreneur Stephen Robinson, 2016.

CELEBRITY SOLVERS

#39

It is a relatively low percentage of the population who can solve a Rubik's Cube, and the number of celebrity solvers is even smaller . . .

Rubik's Cube is a great way to pass the time constructively. You are learning about puzzle solving, following instructions and patterns, among other useful things. Hollywood celebrities are people who often have time on their hands: waiting between takes, hanging out backstage and hiding out on an expansive ranch all provide great opportunities for solving time. Here are a few celebrities who are well known for their Rubik's Cube-solving acumen.

• One of the best-known celebrity solvers is superstar singer Justin Bieber, who has frequently been on television talk shows solving the Cube. He did it while driving and singing as part of Carpool Karaoke in *The Late Late Show* with James Corden, and also on *The Tonight Show* with Jay Leno. Both times he was successful, and he has also

1. Justin Bieber attempts a live solve on television in 2018.
2. Pope Francis sampling the local fare in Budapest, 2023.

been seen on television with a sub-90-second solve time.

• Another famous solver is Will Smith, whose character in *The Pursuit of Happyness* plays with a Rubik's Cube (see page 136). Will is a capable solver himself, however, and has a sub-one-minute televised solve in France.

• Chris Pratt, another Hollywood superstar, is known for his love of the Rubik's Cube, and has been spotted frequently with one on-set and in interviews. Chris – by his own admission – is no speedcuber, but he's a big fan, and his best time is a healthy one minute. On an Instagram post he once wrote, 'Kids who do the Rubik's Cube in under ten seconds are my heroes.' Hopefully one day he will join that elite club.

• The award-winning rapper Logic is proud to describe himself as a 'mixed-race, Rubik's Cube solving, anime-loving rapper'. He sees cubing as one of his key character traits. And of course, he is right – it is something to celebrate.

• Old-school rapper Grandmaster Flash is also a fan of the puzzle, appearing on a *National Geographic* documentary about it, stating, 'Whoever came up with this had to be the geekiest geek of all.'

• Other celebrities have been spotted with Rubik's Cubes, for example Steve Carell, Ryan Gosling and Megan Fox, but it has not been ascertained whether they are capable of solving it or not. Obviously, that does not necessarily matter, for if you can't solve it yet you are still in the learning phase. But David Hasselhoff did admit, 'I have never finished a Rubik's Cube in my life.'

• For American sports fans, NBA superstars Stephen Curry and Chris 'Birdman' Andersen are both avid solvers. Andersen has been involved in educational endeavours where children are encouraged to solve.

• And for football fans (or soccer, as it's known in the USA), Atlético Madrid, Chelsea and Brazil national team player Filipe Luís is a solver. He has appeared on television in Spain – and solving a Rubik's Cube while chatting to his interviewer. Former Manchester City and Spain player David Silva solved a (Manchester City branded) Rubik's Cube for the club's advent calendar.

1. Actress and singer Vanessa Hudgens.

2. Bollywood actor Aamir Khan.

3. Will Smith, mid-solve.

4. Logic solving on television.

CUBE ART

CUBE ART

40

While cubism is an artistic movement from the early twentieth century, Rubik's art is a lot more recent. More often referred to as Rubik's mosaics, this method of creating artwork using cubes has become more popular and established as it has become better known. The medium of mosaic itself dates back thousands of years, but Rubik's mosaics bring the medium right up to date.

An image can be created using only a few Rubik's Cube, but the biggest use tens of thousands. Cubeworks Studio used more than eighty thousand cubes to create the skyline of Macau in China in 2016 – the current Guinness World Record holder for a cube mosaic.

The mural was 65 metres (215 ft) long and 4 metres (13 ft high) and it took six weeks to assemble. Their previous record holder was *The Hand of God*, a re-creation of the image from the Sistine Chapel.

There are individual artists out there too, creating amazing images of all sorts, from sports and rock stars (David Beckham, The Beatles, Elvis) to politicians and famous thinkers (Barack Obama, Einstein), and all sorts of other subjects (portraits, landscapes, logos, maps). The list is endless, as is the creativity applied to making such vivid art using only six colours.

→ Assembling the Macau skyline mural – Cubeworks Studio in 2016.

①

Possibly the most famous solo artist is Invader, known also for his Space Invader street art. He has even collaborated with Rubik's to produce his own Cube: the Rubik's X Invader Limited Edition. Referred to as 'the pioneering artist behind the Rubikcubism movement', Invader is a Paris-based artist whose identity is unknown – in all photos he is wearing a motorcycle helmet or mask. His version of the *Mona Lisa* Rubik's mosaic sold at auction for more than half a million dollars.

Pete Fecteau, an interactive designer from Michigan, USA, built a large cube mosaic entitled *Dream Big*, in 2010. It shows multiple images of Martin Luther King, Jr and was made up of 4,242 cubes. Pete also exhibited a cube mosaic portrait of Ernő Rubik in the Beyond Rubik's Cube exhibition in 2014.

Known as 'The Cubist', Daniella Mani-Chaim created a huge mosaic of NBA superstar Kobe Bryant, after persuading her mother to buy her thousands of cubes – the equivalent of a vast paint supply for the budding cube artist. Daniella has since created many other pieces and says her passion comes from 'art and solving puzzles,' so she is certainly in the right place!

1. Italian artist Giovanni Contardi's image was created for the Red Bull Rubik's Cube World Cup in 2020, using more than six thousand cubes.

2. The mysterious (masked) artist Invader, pictured with some of his artworks – and cubes.

3. Artist Jan Du Plessis created this image of Nelson Mandela out of cubes in South Africa in 2011.

DIGGING
DEEPER

41

**For some, mathematics is horrible;
for others, it is endlessly fascinating.**

For those who are fans, the Rubik's Cube is even more of a joy. While the design of the Rubik's Cube is not based on mathematical principles, mathematics can be applied to the Rubik's Cube in order to discuss group theory. Put simply, this is the study of elements that are present in a group. Sounds simple, right? The Rubik's Cube is a good example because the elements that make up the group are the possible moves that you can make, and the resulting permutations. As we have learned, there are 43 quintillion alternatives (permutations). So, with a finite (albeit massive) number of combinations and a (relatively) small number of moves, the stage is set for some numeric nimbleness of the mind – as well as the fingers.

And just in case your head is getting hot, in the words of Austrian-American mathematician John von Neumann: 'In mathematics you don't understand things. You just get used to them.'

1. Two of the many scientific and mathematical publications.
2. Diagram to show how the elements are rearranged after a single turn (R).

'The Rubik's Cube, a mechanical toy that can be solved using pure mathematics.'

David Joyner, *Adventures in Group Theory*, 2002

①

②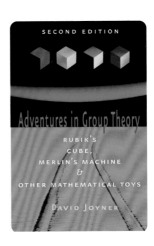

R

CUBE IN THE STREET

42

Professor Rubik did not expect the Cube to become as popular as it did. It is very unlikely that he foresaw the Cube becoming a popular theme in street art either.

Located in Rumbach Street in Budapest, Hungary is a huge patterned painting of a giant Rubik's Cube. In cities all around the world the Rubik's Cube has been used to brighten up streets. These pages showcase just a few of the many cubes to be found.

One notable 'street' cube is located next to the sea at Maroubra Beach in Sydney, Australia (see overleaf). It is, in fact, a storm drain that was transformed by two street artists. Known as the 'Maroubrix Cube' by locals, it was originally painted, in 2008, with an unsolvable colour palette. In 2023, it was redecorated and now resembles a solved cube. Local mayor Philipa Veitch described it as 'a great example of thought-provoking public art.' We wonder if she can solve a regular-sized Rubik's Cube?

➡ Giant street cube in the MuseumsQuartier of Vienna, Austria.

'Rubik's Cubes allow for endless possibilities and variations in the artwork.'

Graffiti Street magazine

A Rubik-kocka
bármely kevésbé után legalább 20 lépésből
kirakható, de az bebizonyítható, hogy döntetlen
43 252 003 274 489 856 000-féle kezdőállásból
áll. 4,3·10¹⁹ ilyen állás lehetséges.

„mindig van megoldás
és nem is csak egy!"
(Rubik Ernő)

BIG-SCREEN

The Rubik's Cube has been a star not only on the small screen, but there are also plenty of films that feature it, either as a symbol of nostalgia or intelligence – sometimes both. Let's look at a number of famous appearances.

Spider-Man: Into the Spider-Verse, 2018

One of the most popular animated movie series of recent years, the Miles Morales Spider-Man series have featured a plethora of different Spider-Men (and women, and creatures). Spider-Man Noir cameos in the first two films of the series and is very interested in the Rubik's Cube. His ability to solve it is complicated, given that he comes from a monochrome world!

Wall·E, 2008

The lonely robot in this Disney/Pixar classic gets stranded on a rubbish-strewn future Earth. One of the abandoned treasures he finds is a Rubik's Cube. Showing the scrambled Cube to his new friend EVE (another robot), WALL·E turns away for a second or two and by the time he returns, EVE has solved it. Now I'm not saying she didn't solve it, I'm just saying you don't actually see her solve it – that wouldn't count in competition!

The Pursuit of Happyness, 2006

Will Smith starred in this touching flim that is based on a real story. In the movie, Smith's character Chris Gardner solves a Rubik's Cube in a taxi, working out how to solve it after seeing it only for a few minutes (his taxi driver also has a scrambled Rubik's Cube). This leads to a job opportunity and, ultimately, to a bright future. (And yes, Gardner can solve a Rubik's Cube IRL.)

Snowden, 2016

The Rubik's Cube features a few times in this film about the ex-CIA and NSA agent. Notably, Snowden hides an SD card in a Rubik's Cube in order to take it to his workplace to download information. In an interesting twist (pun intended), his boss (Nicholas Cage) has a collection of twisty puzzles. The cube takes a prominent place in the trailer.

The Best of the Rest

There are Rubik's Cube featured in many other films, perhaps only as cameos, but usually as an indicator of a character's intelligence.

Interesting examples include: *Interstellar* (2014), *Thor: The Dark World* (2013); *Prometheus* (2012); *Let the Right One In* (*Låt den Rätte Komma In*, 2008); *Hellboy* (2004); *Donnie Darko* (2001); *Being John Malkovich* (1999); *Armageddon* (1998); and finally *Dude, Where's My Car?* (2000), which goes to prove that there are exceptions to the intellectual theme.

1. *Let the Right One In* – a dark tale of friendship set in Sweden.

2. Owen Wilson and Vince Vaughn puzzle it out in *The Internship* (2013).

CUBE **RECORDS**   **#44**

There are many records relating to cubing.
Everyone has a personal best, even if that's just the
fastest time to solve one layer. Here are just a few
of the big solving records.

Fastest 3x3 Cube Solve: Max Park **3.13** seconds (single)
Fastest 3x3 Cube Solve: Yiheng Wang* **4.48** seconds (average)

Fastest One-handed 3x3 Cube Solve: Max Park **6.2** seconds (single)
Fastest One-handed 3x3 Cube Solve: Sean Patrick Villanueva **8.09** seconds. (av.)

Fewest moves 3x3 Cube Solve: Sebastiano Tronto: **16** (single)
Fewest moves 3x3 Cube Solve: Wong Chong Wen: **20** (average)

Fastest Blindfolded 3x3 Cube Solve: Tommy Cherry **12** seconds (single)
Fastest Blindfolded 3x3 Cube Solve: Tommy Cherry **14.15** seconds (average)

Fastest 2x2 Cube Solve: Teodor Zajder **0.43** seconds (single)
Fastest 2x2 Cube Solve: Zayn Khanani **0.92** seconds (average)

Fastest 4x4 Cube Solve: Max Park **15.83** seconds (single)
Fastest 4x4 Cube Solve: Max Park **19.38** seconds (average)

Fastest 5x5 Cube Solve: Max Park **32.52** seconds (single)
Fastest 5x5 Cube Solve: Max Park **35.94** seconds (average)

⬆ School children in London making a – successful – attempt at the group solving world record in 2012. The event raised money for homeless charities.

*Yiheng Wang was nine years old at the time.

ERNŐ RUBIK

#45

We've learned how the Rubik's Cube works, how popular it has been around the world and how the desire to solve it faster took decades. What about the man behind the machine?

Professor Ernő Rubik is a curious man. That is to say he is filled with curiosity; he likes to seek answers and solutions. He was a professor of design at the Academy of Applied Arts and Design in Budapest in the 1970s, when he developed his first Cube. Ever since he was young (he was born in 1944, at the end of the Second World War), he had an interest in designing and creating shapes and he spent a lot of time building them out of paper, cardboard and wood. When he had built that first Cube, he did not even envisage that it would have a use as a puzzle – he just wanted to create a work of art.

Fortunately for us, Rubik was able to see the object's worth as a puzzle, and it rapidly went on to become one of the bestselling puzzles – and one of the bestselling toys – of all time.

Cubes were originally assembled in Hungary, where the country's

➡ Professor Rubik in front of an array of twisty puzzles, *c*.2010.

140

'It speaks to the universal values in human nature: curiosity, perseverance, and ingenuity.'

Professor Ernő Rubik, describing the Cube

Communist doctrine meant that free-market economics, as practised in the West, could not be observed. So, it was a Hungarian company, Politechnika, that was the first to sell the Cube until companies in the West were allowed to build and sell it. Soon after, Rubik's Cubes were made in China.

A few years after the Rubik's Cube became really popular, Rubik opened his own design studio, which quickly began to release new, innovative products, including many more 'twisty puzzles', as they have become known.

He is responsible for hundreds of other twisty puzzles. This category did not even exist before his creation, but now it features in toy shops and supermarkets everywhere. There are bigger, smaller and more complicated puzzles in the style of the Rubik's Cube, but all relate to the one he made fifty years ago.

'The Rubik's Cube is a piece of art. It comes to life when we attempt to discover our own solutions to the vast complexity of the challenge,' he said. The challenge has lasted half a century, and counting!

At the World Rubik's Cube Championship in 2007, Professor Rubik said to *Time* magazine, 'I'm glad the cube is reaching new generations who face it with fresh wonder, curiosity and enthusiasm.' He was right at the time, and the sentiment is still correct today.

As if to demonstrate his enduring curiosity and thirst for knowledge and love of discovery, Rubik is still an inventor, architect, designer, editor, and writer.

← Covers of Professor Rubik's 2020 book, *Cubed: The Puzzle of Us All*.

RESURGENCE

#46

After hitting massive heights of popularity upon launch, the Rubik's Cube went out of the limelight for a while. But it was too good a puzzle to simply disappear – and it came back with a bang.

By 1982, the Rubik's Cube was less popular – hardly surprising given the explosion of popularity it had enjoyed. *The New York Times* declared it 'passé'. But the Cube was 'far too eternal, far too amazing a structure, for people to lose interest in it,' said long-lasting fan Douglas Hofstadter.

He was right: the turn of the century saw a massive resurgence in popularity. Sales increased, competitions restarted and, as *The Boston Globe* said, it was 'cool to own a Cube again.'

It was the age of the supercuber. Solving times plummeted, and the World Cube Association welcomed new competitors all over the world.

The emergence of the 'cuberstars' helped the Cube make its way back into the global psyche, with appearances in films, television shows and music videos, as well as bookshops and toy stores.

The longevity of a Rubik's Cube (they easily outlast video games), its tactile nature and the endless challenge on offer shows the Rubik's Cube is really here to stay.

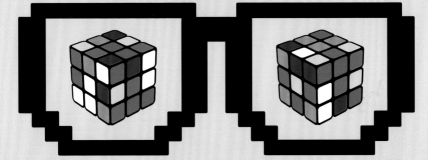

GEEK

IS THE NEW

CHIC

TIMELINE

47

The Cube has been with us for more than fifty years. This timeline highlights the key events along the way.

1974 — Rubik creates his first Cube, the 3x3 prototype.

1977 — First 'Magic Cubes' are sold in Hungary.

1979 — International distribution deal with Ideal Toys.

1980 — The 'Magic Cube' becomes the Rubik's Cube.

1981 — Rubik's Cube is awarded Toy of the Year.

1981 — The first Guinness World Record time for solving a Rubik's Cube is set: 38 seconds.

1981 — *You Can Do the Cube* becomes a global bestseller.

1982 — First international Rubik's Cube Championships.

1982		World record solving time of 22.95 seconds.
1991		The Rubik's Cube is featured in *The Simpsons* – not for the last time!
1997		The Fridrich method of solving is published.
2003		The World Cube Association is founded and the first world championships since 1982 take place.
2006		Will Smith's character in *The Pursuit of Happyness* famously solves a Rubik's Cube.
2008		A Rubik's Cube is featured in the Disney/Pixar hit *Wall•E*.
2008		'You Can Do the Cube' STEM school programme launched in the USA.
2012		A new record is set for simultaneous solving, by 1,414 children in London, England.
2014		The Rubik's Cube celebrates its 40th anniversary.

2014		The *Beyond Rubik's* exhibition is launched.
2015		The first verified solving time of under 5 seconds.
2015		Justin Bieber solves a cube live on television.
2017		Feliks Zemdegs solves a cube in new record time (4.73 seconds).
2018		The first verified solving time of under 4 seconds is recorded.
2018		A robot solves a cube in 0.38 secs.
2020		Ernő Rubik releases *Cubed: The Puzzle of Us All*.
2020		Forty years since the first Rubik's Cube was sold.
2023		Max Park solves in a new record time: 3.13 sec.
2024		50th anniversary of the Rubik's Cube; special edition Cube released.

➡ Advertising the Rubik's Cube throughout the decades.

FINGER TRICKING: #48
GET UP TO SPEED

The fastest solving solutions require the fastest fingers. Finger tricking is all about moving the Rubik's Cube as fast as you possibly can.

As you now know, becoming a speedcuber involves mental as well as physical prowess. Once you have chosen your preferred solving method and learned the myriad algorithms (easier said than done – but a great challenge to overcome!) you will need to ensure you are turning, twisting and rotating your cube as fast as you possibly can.

You will have noticed how Uncle Richard picks up the Rubik's Cube and turns a few sides as if he is a bit scared it will pop open like a jack-in-the-box, but you will need to be more nimble and dexterous in order to get your times down to the best you can possibly manage. And that is where finger tricking comes in.

Rather than moving your hand to one side and turning a face of the cube, with finger tricking you use your fingers (and thumb) to push the parts side to side or up and down.

Remember: Finger tricking is a skill, and that means you will need to practice in order to improve. Here are a few of the basics . . .

We are going to assume you know basic cube notation (see page 78).

R and L moves (right/left faces)

To execute fast R moves, hold the right face of the cube with your thumb on the bottom and your fingers on the top. Spin your right wrist to make the move. For R', reverse the direction, gripping the back with your fingers and the top front with the thumb. Note that L moves will be the same, but using left hand and wrist.

U moves (up face)

Use your fore (index) fingers to push the top layer. Push with your right finger (U) or your left finger (U').

D moves (down face)

These can be executed with your little (pinkie) finger or your ring finger, while your other fingers and thumbs grip the cube, making sure you don't allow the middle layer to move too.

B moves (back face)

These moves will usually require a repositioning of the cube in your hands (towards you), and will then be done with your fore (index) fingers, as with the up face (see left).

F moves (front face)

One way to do this is to re-grip the cube – moving the front face upwards – and then use your index fingers to move it as with moves for that face (right finger U, left U'). Alternatively you can use your thumbs to turn the face as you grip the cube with your other fingers.

RESOURCES   #49

Where do I find out more? The Rubik's Cube features in hundreds of thousands of articles, apps, programmes and more – it's not hard to find information and help.

I f you want to learn more about the Cube, there are many, many resources online. Step-by-step instructions, videos, histories, mathematical theses and a *lot* of solves can be found. Here are some interesting sites:

The Official Rubik's
Rubiks.com
This is the parent site of the Cube's creator and a real treasure trove of everything to do with the Rubik's Cube. You'll find some of the clearest

solving guides out there, plenty of history and other information, and section all about finger tricks, with 3D animations for all sorts of moves.

csTimer
cstimer.net
This site contains cube-scrambling algorithms that are straightforward and easy to follow, as well as stats functions and solving tools, not to mention the timer!

Feliks and Max

Feliksandmax.com

This site brings together two of the best speedcubers of all time: Feliks Zemdegs and Max Park. There are videos and other information from the world record holders.

Ruwix

Ruwix.com

This site contains all sorts of information related to the Rubik's Cube, from history and solving techniques to amusing images and cube art.

SpeedCubeDB

speedcubedb.com

This site features plenty of solving tips for all sorts of cubes and other twisty puzzles, as well as interesting algorithms you may not easily find elsewhere. You can track your learning progress, read reviews and learn all about a huge variety of solving techniques.

SpeedSolving

speedsolving.com

If you want to share and talk to your fellow Rubik's Cube solvers, this is the place to do it. A fascinating, fun, friendly puzzle community awaits!

World Cube Association

Worldcubeassociation.org

This official site contains details of all competitions (upcoming and historical) and lists the current and historical world records, as well as regulations, results and a forum. It is a mine of useful information for the pro speedcuber.

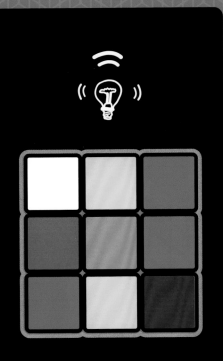

NOT A CUBE?

#50

When is a Cube not a Cube? When it is a stress ball, a notepad or a cake! Here we look at objects that look like Rubik's Cubes – but they can't be twisted or turned.

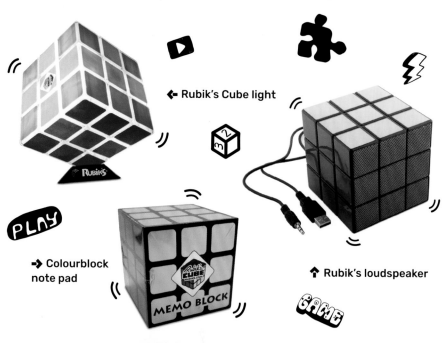

← Rubik's Cube light

→ Colourblock note pad

↑ Rubik's loudspeaker

Cube bag

Rubik's Foam Cube

CUBE DOES NOT TWIST

Rubik's

SQUISHABLE FOAM CUBE

Cube dessert

Rubik's Cube Bank

BIBLIOGRAPHY

Adams, William Lee, 'The Rubik's Cube: A Puzzling Success, 28 January 2009, *Time magazine.*

Alter, Alexandra, 'He Invented the Rubik's Cube. He's Still Learning From It', *The New York Times*, 16 September 2020.

amNY, 'Kids graffiti Astor cube and get collared by police', *The Villager*, 11 April 2006.

Babych, Stephanie, 'World's largest Rubik's Cube takes a spin at Telus Spark, *Calgary Herald*, 22 August 2018.

Bandelow, Christoph, *Inside Rubik's Cube and Beyond*, translated by Jeannette Zehnder and Lucy Moser, Birkhäuser, 1982.

Behar, Jack and Dardashty, 'Milken Freshman Daniella Mani-Chaim: Creating Art One Rubik's Cube at a Time', 7 May 2021, *The Roar*.

Borders, William, 'Best-Selling Author, 13, Thanks Rubik's Cube, *The New York Times*, 16 October 1981.

Chen, Janet, 'Group Theory and the Rubik's Cube'. people.math.harvard.edu/~jjchen/docs/Group%20 Theory%20and%20the%20Rubik's%20Cube.pdf

Cornish, Ruby, 'The mystery of Maroubra's Rubik's Cube has been solved but locals are divided on its new look', ABC News, 16 December 2023.

Donna, 'Rubikcubism: A captivating and innovative art movement by Invader, 2023', *Graffiti Street*, 22 September 2022.

Fish, Iliana, 'Cubism 2.0 – Daniella Mani Chaim', *JLiving*, 19 March 2023.

Fridrich, Jessica, 'My system for solving Rubik's Cube', www.ws.binghamton.edu/fridrich/system.html

Hofstadter, Douglas R., 'Metamagical Themas: The Magic Cube's cubies are twiddled by cubists and solved by cubemeisters', *Scientific American*, March 1981.

Jaffa, Jacob, 'Puzzling Task' in *The Sun*, 7 March.

Joyner, David, *Adventures in Group Theory: Rubik's Cube, Merlin's Machine and Other Mathematical Toys*, The Johns Hopkins University Press, Baltimore and London, 2002.

Joyner, W. D., *Mathematics of the Rubik's Cube*, www.fuw.edu.pl/~konieczn/RubikCube.pdf

Marx, George, 'For me, the cube is an object of nature', An interview with Erno Rubik, *Impact of Science on Society*, Vol. 32, No. 4, 1982.

Matheson, Whitney 'Forty years later, the Rubik's Cube still puzzles', *USA Today*, 25 April 2014.

Mulholland, Jamie, *Permutation Puzzles: A Mathematical Perspective*. www.sfu.ca/~jtmulhol/ math302/

Nadler, John, 'Squaring Up to the Rubik's Cube, *Time magazine*, 9 October 2007.

pjk, 'Interview with Jessica Fridrich and Zbigniew Zborowski about Feliks Zemdegs', 20 April 2020.

Reese, Hope, 'The Unlikely Endurance of the Rubik's Cube', *Undark*, 23 September, 2020.

Reese, Hope, 'A Brief History of the Rubik's Cube, *Undark, Smithsonian Magazine*, 25 September 2020.

Rubik, Ernö, Varga, Tamás, Kéri, Gerzson, Marx, György and Vekerdy, Tamás, *Rubik's Cubic Compendium*, translation edited by David Singmaster, Oxford University Press, 1987.

Simpson, Dave, 'Erno Rubik: how we made the Rubik's Cube', *The Guardian*, 26 May 2015.

Sly, David, 'Behind the design of the d'Arenberg Cube', *Gourmet Traveller*, 25 June, 2018.

www.cubelelo.com/

'God's Number is 20': cube20.org.

'Group Theory', BYJU's, byjus.com/group-theory/

'An interview with Rubik's Cube creator Ernő Rubik' by Guinness World Records, 13 July 2021.

On this Day, in 1974: the "Magic Cube" was invented by Ernő Rubik. *Kafkadesk* Budapest, 19 May 2021.

'The Perplexing Life of Erno Rubik' www.puzzlesolver.com/puzzle.php?id=29&page=15.

Rubik's Cube, How Products are Made.

Rubik's Cubes in the Movies rubikscubesinmovies.com/

Rubik's Cube Lifecycle, designlife-cycle.com

'Rubik's robot solves puzzle in 0.38 seconds', BBC.com, 8 March 2018.

ruwix.com

Solving the Rubik's Cube, *National Geographic*, 2014, www.youtube.com/watch?v=Mlejkn807NI.

ukspeedcubes.co.uk/

World Cube Association www.worldcubeassociation.org/

CREDITS

First published in 2024 by White Lion Publishing
An imprint of The Quarto Group.
1 Tryptych Place, 185 Park Street,
London, SE1 9SH, United Kingdom
T (0)20 7700 6700
www.quarto.com

A catalogue record for this book is available from the British Library.

ISBN 978-0-7112-9827-9
eBook ISBN 978-0-7112-9828-6

10 9 8 7 6 5 4 3 2 1

Printed in China

FSC
www.fsc.org
MIX
Paper | Supporting responsible forestry
FSC® C008047

Tom Nicholson/Huawei 85BL; Whitney Shefte/The Washington Post 103T; Michael Macor/The San Francisco Chronicle 105B; Paul Drinkwater/NBC/NBCU Photo Bank 117L; Gary Gershoff/WireImage for Ruth C. Schwartz and Co., Inc 118TL; Prodip Guha/Hindustan Times 118TR; Vera Anderson/WireImage 118BL; Douglas Gorenstein/NBCU Photo Bank/NBCUniversal 118BR; Gregory Bojorquez 123; Foto24/Gallo Images 125; Alexi Rosenfeld 130BR; David Collier 131; YOSHIKAZU TSUNO/AFP 157BL. **Graphisoft Park**: www.graphisoftpark.hu 86TL, 86TR. **Johns Hopkins University Press**: 127R. **Muza S.A.**, Poland: 142L. **National Museum of American History**/Smithsonian Institution: 73. **Nina Mall**, Hong Kong, China: 83. **Puffin Books**: 77R. **Stephen Robinson**: 115B. *Scientific American*: 21. **Shutterstock**: Olga Popova 9BR; Ted Thai/The LIFE Picture Collection 11; F16-ISO100 52; Mikael Buck 65; Yoshio Tsunoda/AFLO 71BL; newfreehanded 97; Julian Smith/EPA 103BL; Mike Hollist/ANL 113; ABACA 117R; Attila Husejnow/SOPA Images 133; Ray Tang 139; HelloRF Zcool 157BR. **Speedcubing Canada**: 105TR. **Unesco**: 127L. **Unsplash**: Julian Paolo Dayag 85BR; Jiawei Luo 110TR; Sven de Koe 110BR. **Illustration by Toma Vagner**: 59. **Wikimedia Commons**: Filip Bart_omiej Perkowski 38; Euku 68R; Globetrotter 19, 86BR; Schneelocke 81C.